Cicadas

by Christina Leaf

BLASTOFF! READERS

BELLWETHER MEDIA • MINNEAPOLIS, MN

Note to Librarians, Teachers, and Parents:

Blastoff! Readers are carefully developed by literacy experts and combine standards-based content with developmentally appropriate text.

Level 1 provides the most support through repetition of high-frequency words, light text, predictable sentence patterns, and strong visual support.

Level 2 offers early readers a bit more challenge through varied simple sentences, increased text load, and less repetition of high-frequency words.

Level 3 advances early-fluent readers toward fluency through increased text and concept load, less reliance on visuals, longer sentences, and more literary language.

Level 4 builds reading stamina by providing more text per page, increased use of punctuation, greater variation in sentence patterns, and increasingly challenging vocabulary.

Level 5 encourages children to move from "learning to read" to "reading to learn" by providing even more text, varied writing styles, and less familiar topics.

Whichever book is right for your reader, Blastoff! Readers are the perfect books to build confidence and encourage a love of reading that will last a lifetime!

This edition first published in 2018 by Bellwether Media, Inc.

No part of this publication may be reproduced in whole or in part without written permission of the publisher. For information regarding permission, write to Bellwether Media, Inc., Attention: Permissions Department, 5357 Penn Avenue South, Minneapolis, MN 55419.

Library of Congress Cataloging-in-Publication Data

Names: Leaf, Christina.
Title: Cicadas / by Christina Leaf.
Description: Minneapolis, MN : Bellwether Media, Inc., 2018. | Series: Blastoff! Readers. Insects Up Close | Audience: Ages 5-8. | Audience: K to grade 3. | Includes bibliographical references and index.
Identifiers: LCCN 2016055092 (print) | LCCN 2017004925 (ebook) | ISBN 9781626176607 (hardcover : alk. paper) | ISBN 9781681033907 (ebook)
Subjects: LCSH: Cicadas–Juvenile literature.
Classification: LCC QL527.C5 L43 2018 (print) | LCC QL527.C5 (ebook) | DDC 595.7/52–dc23
LC record available at https://lccn.loc.gov/2016055092

Editor: Christina Leighton   Designer: Maggie Rosier

Printed in the United States of America, North Mankato, MN.

Table of Contents

What Are Cicadas?

Cicadas make a lot of noise. They are the loudest insects in the world!

Some cicadas
are dark with red
eyes. Others have
green marks.

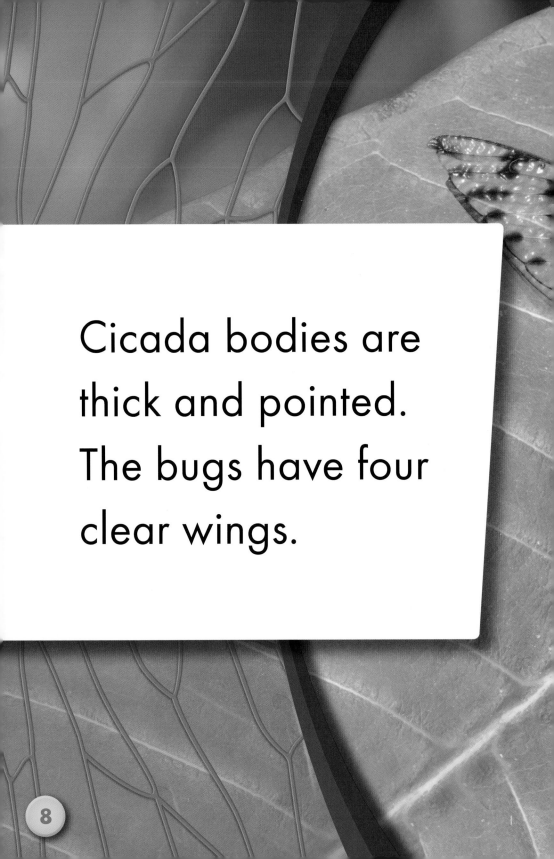

Cicada bodies are thick and pointed. The bugs have four clear wings.

ACTUAL SIZE:

17-year cicada

wings

9

Tree Life

Cicadas like warm summers. Most live in forests.

FAVORITE FOOD:

tree sap

A male buzzes to find females. **Tymbals** on his **abdomen** move quickly to make noise.

abdomen

tymbals

13

A female digs a line in a tree branch. She lays eggs there.

14

female
cicada

eggs

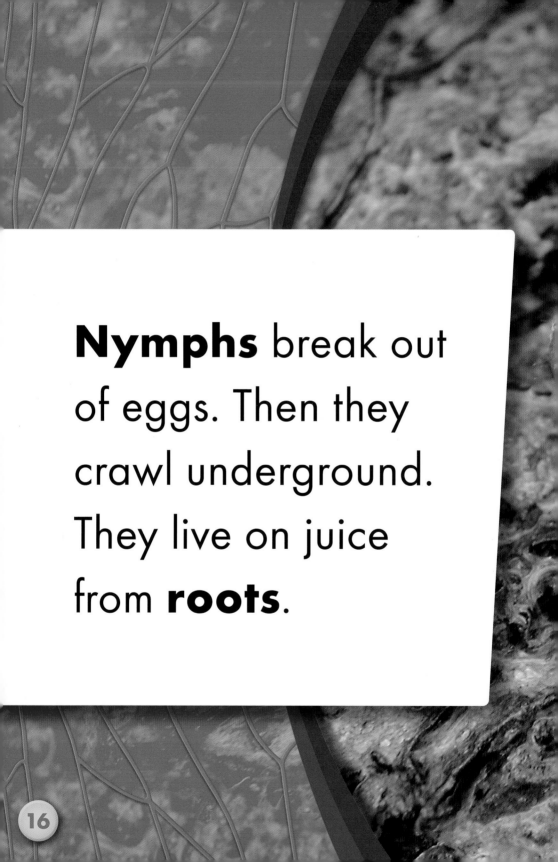

Nymphs break out of eggs. Then they crawl underground. They live on juice from **roots**.

nymph

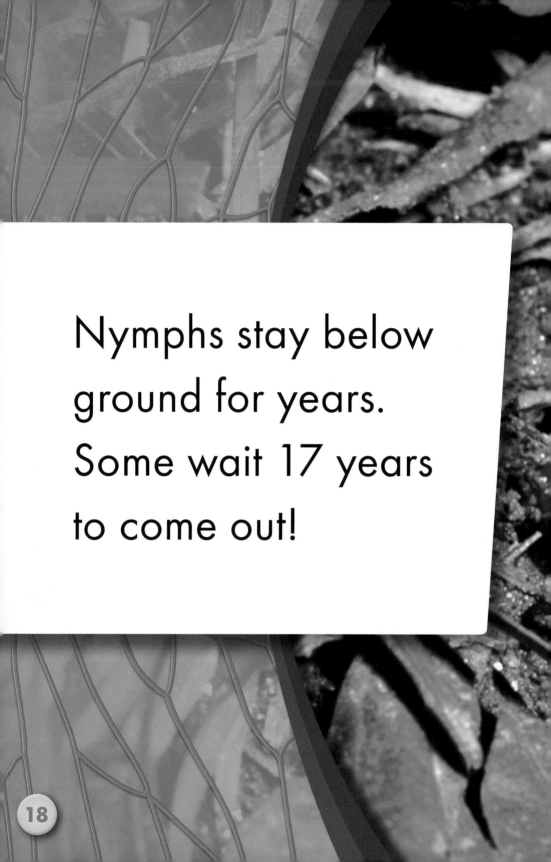

Nymphs stay below ground for years. Some wait 17 years to come out!

CICADA
LIFE SPAN:

up to 17 years

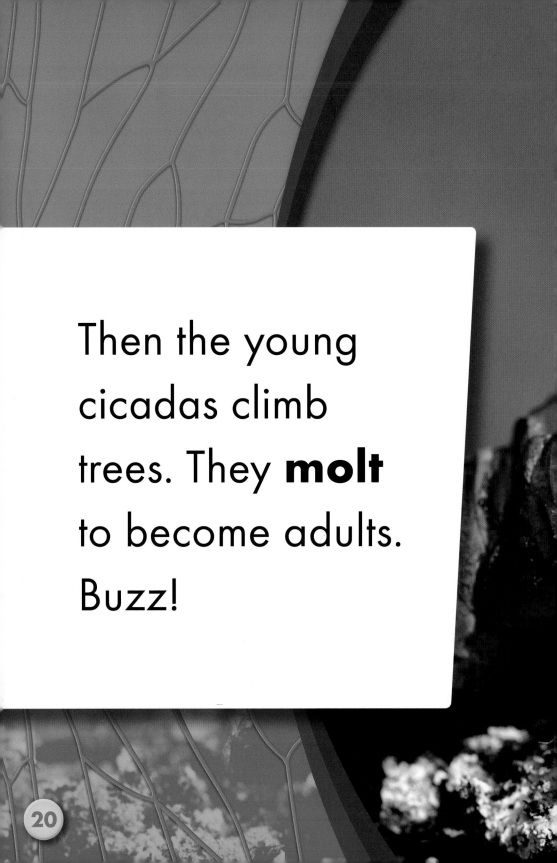

Then the young cicadas climb trees. They **molt** to become adults. Buzz!

molting

Glossary

abdomen

the back part of an insect's body

roots

the underground parts of plants that take in water and store food

molt

to shed skin for growth

tymbals

thin parts on a cicada's abdomen that buzz by moving back and forth

nymphs

young insects; nymphs look like small adults without full wings.

To Learn More

AT THE LIBRARY

Amstutz, Lisa J. *Cicadas*. North Mankato, Minn.: Capstone Press, 2014.

Buellis, Linda. *Cicadas*. New York, N.Y.: PowerKids Press, 2017.

Schuh, Mari. *Cicadas*. Minneapolis, Minn.: Jump!, 2015.

ON THE WEB
Learning more about cicadas is as easy as 1, 2, 3.

1. Go to www.factsurfer.com.

2. Enter "cicadas" into the search box.

3. Click the "Surf" button and you will see a list of related web sites.

With factsurfer.com, finding more information is just a click away.

Index

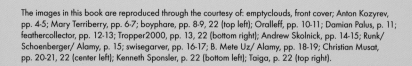